Essay On Pope

Richard Blevins

to Rev. Zac Derr

The visit to London is our visit to Pythia.
—Gilles Deleuze

DORN — WASHED UP ON AN ISLAND IN TIME

SPUYTEN DUYVIL
New York City

ISBN 978-1-963908-75-6

artwork/t thilleman

Library of Congress Control Number: 2025936441

ARGUMENT

Edward Dorn and an American scholar have agreed to meet in London on the 300th anniversary of Alexander Pope's birth. Due to the formal nature and current conditions of Poetry and Scholarship, the two miss connections—Dorn participating in ceremonies at Pope's Tomb; and our narrator the Gloomy Clerk arriving at the Grotto. Antonin Artaud engineers a conceptual Bridge between the oppositions of life or death.

A "Dorn" is a thorn like Pope, in the side.
Bernofsky's "A thorn gets stuck in an eye."

Society can carry the form'r
Around for a long while like a thin book;
Eyes require immediate attention.

I.

Only the De Form'd are beautiful.
To light at St Mary's, Cross Deep,
as if the 300th candle on Pope's Cake,
Ed Dorn lands
for the exhumation.
"Be that my task too,"
the Gloomy Clerk in me chimed.
To de-form my language, I assumed:
Dorn was not, strictly speaking,
OK'd to take off—
he was already arrived by Turbine,
on the winds of having perfected the interview form,
form kept the engine idling
in the blue shade of his Stetson,
thumbing through a paperback Sky
waiting for me to catch up.
Flight is levitation in Cendrars,
still his miner remembers to carry
a bird on his shoulder
to test the caverns' air,
sky no longer. "There is no creature,"
he reads,
"who is so alien to this world
as the bird,
for where is the graveyard,
the ossuary of the birds?"
Cendrars did his homework

to write the history
of ecstatic levitation, 1000-1913.
Dorn is what we have of a living AP
come all the way to earth to experience
Death.
He could have saved himself
the trip—having written
"Death rules over the visible."
I skipped classes and watched Watergate
on his TV. "To study the hierarchies,"
Dorn had lived in England. I know
he would figure the Grotto
for where Pope kept Charles' first head.
Bleary Traveler,
Tenure is here for you.
To comfort you in your cynicism with offers,
Of fresh mouths in genderless rooms,
walled with books from before Britain became
a colony of Amerika,
when it was all English lit, though
you are acutely aware
all tenured dunces have the Bug,
and drinking each other's tears
is bound to infect.
For my two-handed eulogy,
I have prepared Whitman's line
from the deathbed *Leaves*,
"To die is different from what anyone supposed,
and luckier,"
pleading Lucky Strikes ignorance

to Form and its Alities.
The college sent Jeremy Bentham to the airport
("I came on the heels of Pope, and I'm still here!"}
with a car and a check. I easily ditched Jeremy: drove off
leaving him in a shop buying cigarettes he didn't need.
Lucky my horror of
death by driving on the wrong side of the road
is put to rest
by the MLA's CIA-funded motorcade
to Pope's Grotto, Twickenham.
Traffic lights and small cars meant nothing to me;
I was driving behind the hearse of Hierarchy
According to The Fieve Orders of Perriwigs,
Curll's Merryland spread open like a map.
A sea of cars parted before my urge
only to crash behind my passage;
a child with blazing eyes sat on the bonnet
as a warning to others that we were behind Pope.
Then came the calamity.

My eyes have adjusted to the stained glass,
But I still can't see you, Ed.

My willful misreading has him and Xem
driving off in two directions.

II. THE FLIGHT (DORN)

This garden is going to be difficult to destroy.
"Manchester Square"

…I plainly see from 40,000 feet
Economics is Parmenides' Whole,
The hole Digger fell into like a grave.
See the north sea closes below my seat.
This chariot to Sophie is a jet
To Heathrow; Odysseus left Calypso
On a raft handmade from fistfuls of Dorns.
Pope translates the passage: "Strong with the fear
Of death. In rolling flood, / Now here, now there,
Impell'd the floating wood / As when a heap
Of gather'd thorns [ie, Dorns] is cast."
Airmail from Parmenides just circles
Since Zeno became his Secretary.
…Parmenides was the first to locate
The Morning Star—he also mistook it
For The Evening Star…My carry-on
"Proem" declar's Truth is the One Big Deal;
The Confidence Man taught me the biggest
Thing is one man's
"Trust," it makes the economy turn on
Its axes, and yet each man has his price,
Can be bot, so the plot is he holds out
To sell out in his own good time. Picking
Up baggage that comes around in customs.

When I go traditional, I am more
So than Pope: I wrote The Shoshoneans,
And a cycle of love songs to Her.
(A Scriblerean-like newspaper Bean.)
Mostly packing suitcase poems for the flight.
…Lust for Calypso kept him seen years
In Paradise—the surprise is for Pope
To uphold Homer's formula
Instead of seeing the Cave as Grotto.
Seven years can be a stretch in any
Direction, including too far and out.
The build: Atlantic Turbine to Slinger
Occupi'd seven years; duration
In the Tenure Cave as Calypso's guest
(her name means "she who conceals knowledge"),
Crafting, piece by piece, a more modest raft,
Peeling oars from trees, diplomas for sails.
The goddess promis'd what she could not De-
Liver—immortality. Ezra Pound
Was wrong—to live in paradise is not
Immortality. That makes Jimmy Joyce
Right: "Calypso" concerns economics.
Beginning in the management of Greek
Households, amounting to *economy*
Of language. Even Bloom's cat "understands
All she wants to. Vindictive too. Cruel,"
A Calypso the likes of Daniel Drew.
…Pope! What Truth do I seek at your flat tomb?
Can I confirm, in dust, facility
In writing is not facile, and hating

A hater cannot go out of fashion.

Mature Pope is a capitalist just

Before the South Seas Bubble crash he cash'd

Stock, financ'd his Villa, Grounds, and Grotto.

Walpole return'd 6% on the pound.

Speculation cost Newton a fortune.

Investment that grew the slave trade acts

According to Newton's unwritten Lawe:

Ethics is the cost of doing Business.

(During the South Seas Co. crisis,

Isaac Newton the Master of the Mint

Pursu'd counterfeiters like Chalones,

Like Ezra the son's dream of Homer Pound.)

Divest Thyself 'fore the Turbine brakes

On your best enemy's winning number,

Turning all friendships into transactions!

There is no money in poems. Only

A series of teaching positions

During the printing of the fourth *Dunciad*,

Fine pages it took a knife to cut,

and the abandonment of his Grotto,

Pope declined Oxford's offer,

"Isis and Cam made Doctors of [Dulness'] Laws,"

Vaillant swallow'd his medals and served them

with Spinach for two meals running.

I faithfully remain cool to the poems as verse,

adverse to aphorisms for the stereosexual;

yet awestruck that the massive dumping of language

could signal the unstopped roar of

all the loose water on the planet. And how

strange unto appropriate for late

Capitalism to cover this distance from Adam Smith

only to discover wildfire Artaud

repatriated, our saint and tourist guide

to the Grave of Pope. Strange as the deformed

poet's dream of stretching his legs on a walk.

Artaud moves more variously

than when he was only mad. He himself

punched our tickets, like front teeth in a bar fight,

slyly pocketing the change.

The parade he led into the church yard

was one controlled series of violent excavations,

my tooled boots pulled from mud-suck over

the backs and liquid faces of the dead.

("First he relates, how sinking to the chin,

Smit with his mien, the mud-nymphs suck'd him in").

Public speculation on the size

of Mr. Pope's YARD, slang for the penis,

drove up his book sales!   Churlish

Curll names his print shop Pope's Head.

They grow erect; I, all the more correct.

I am the deformed poet aroused by voluptuous hierarchies

The Desire to be a member (14 portraits in the Scriblerian's house)

Wm Trumbull II writes "He looked & really was

No more than a shadow," the year

He met Martha Blount. Amica

Was a fan so enamored of Pope, "I have indeed placc'd Mr. Pope in every Room in my Apartments," 1737 to 1744,

he had to ask her to desist, the exact years he was placing materials in the third Grotto.

"I'm not a real person, just the shit

you can't make up," Will Wood.

Pope was a lifelong patient
Like Coleridge, Wyndham Lewis, Eigner, Patchen

"This child
is not there,
he is but an angle,
an angle to come,
and there is no angle…,"
Artaud tells us, as if he'd lifted it from somewhere.

Cheselden, the surgeon who helped Pope
edit *Romeo and Juliet,*
might have cut higher, removed a rib
so Pope could turn his neck again, look
around and kiss, was content with Strangury.

The sculptor Roubiliac observed,
in 1738, Pope's face
had the look of a man with a headache.

Pope to Bethel, Feb. 20, 1744:
"I am grown so tender as not to be able
to feel the air, or get out
of a multitude of Waistcoats.
I live like an Insect, in hope of
reviving with the Spring…"
He often likened himself to a spider.
Sleepless, exhausted: he treated himself
with coffee inhalations. Was prescribed
a diet of asses' milk. The last book

Pope read was Bishop Berkeley's Treatise
on the tar-water cure Berkeley had learned
in Rhode Island.

Dame Sitwell's little life of Pope ends: "But he lies at peace, although
the geese cackled and the jackals whined over his grave." No wild animals

around today, only the human kind.
Rumor mongers and critics.

((I'm never alone
Cannot dress myself
I cultivate enemies, name names,
That hump on my back is a gun.
I learned manners in tombs
I lived in the Cave of Adullam,
Abishag kept warm my bosom.
I am her afterlife of perfectly used Verbs, her off-the-shoulder shroud
My disfigurement curls me in on myself.
I installed
Drains in the Grotto floor
For the blood.))

At the flat grave now, familiar as Minnesota:
The Aubrey holes sunk into this land/…the dropped H/and glottic T/as suspended in time.
Portraits turned to the wall.
Sitwell recalls the less familiar
Pope telling the vain painter Kneller he wished to be buried
"wherever I drop;
most likely Twitnam."

Aubrey's portraits,

Plain and unframed,

Anticipate modernity

As does Dunciad IV

unveil metabook form

To include fictive critical commentary, scholarly apparatus such as mock footnotes, appendices, prefaces, errata,

ghosted testimonials, & so forth.

Pope among Blake and Smart.

Still we must imitate the minor poets

when we write.

Coleridge credits Wm. Bowles for reviving

the sonnet form.

…Bowles published his thin poems, and an edition of Pope. Later attacked by the Popeans and Byron.

I left,

when the madman broke the restraining ring of paid mourners

and he dove, weeping, into

the reopened Question

grave fresh lined with peonies and allium, the widow without a corpse

to kiss, left to rot in her king's tomb,

I turned away. Meaning to walk the short space to my hotel.

Hoping I could keep the Thames

in sight. There is no money in poems.

My desire is to be / a classical poet.

III. THE GLOOMY CLERK ESSAYS

"If you get there first, put a chalk mark."
"What if you get there first?"
"Then I'll rub it out!"
Moe to Larry, *Three Little Pigskins*

Abstract

Deleuze and Guattari,
reading Artaud, propose
there are three stages
in developing the body without organs:
    A. The Empty
    B. The Full
    C. The Cancerous.
Their BwO is many actions
toward an unobtainable goal,
including assemblages.
The BwO must aim to become all potential
by disposing of categorization (A);
and be pure intensity (B), although this
also creating new limits to potential;
the Cancerous (C) is overly elaborated
and includes echolalia.
  These stages are exemplified
in Pope's
versions of the Grotto 1725,
1739, and 1744.*

*Japan made a video game out of it.

The 1725 Grotto

"…When you shut the Doors of the Grotto, it becomes on the instant,
from a luminous Room, a *Camera obscura*; on the Walls of which the
Objects of the River, Hills, Woods, and Boats, are moving forming a
Moving Picture in their visible Radiations: And when you have a mind
to light it up, it affords you a very different Scene; it is finished with
Shells interspersed with Pieces of Looking-glass in angels forms; and
in the Ceiling is a Star of the same Material, at which when a Lamp (of
an orbicular Figure of thin Alabaster) is hung in the Middle, a thousand pointed
Rays glitter and are reflected over the Place."
Pope letter, from 1725.

Horace,
the Amerikan emeritus who resembled a talking Horse,
was seriously hilarious
in his unbridled attempt at nonchalance.
Chews gum at the lectern, both hooves deep
into pants pockets, when a passing bug drone
flew in his mouth,
he lost his page
and pulled out twin waterfalls in a relfex
of loose change.
I don't understand his books
are never funny.
I did not dare look at Kidd, whose books of poems are fun
That day, slapstick beat satire.
In a gesture toward decorum,

by now an almost exclusively
academic notion
formerly called Cool,
no one came forward
to pick up the coins from the floor.
I spoke next! "Thank you, doctor,
for the introduction…"
Years later, I learned
about the faculty meeting
when he rose to his full height
and proposed half his salary
to hire an instructor.

  The guide addresses a tight circle
of tourists inside Mammoth Cave.
Everyone becomes aware of pressure
on their heads, when the guide
turns off the lights for the moment
Floyd Collins kicks over his lamp
Eyes try to adjust to total darkness,
While Kleitman sleeps.

In the early years, perhaps Pope could retreat to the Grotto, and even compose in solitude as imagined in Wm Kent's sketch "Pope at work in the grotto." Initially, Pope ponders the stage one Emptiness of the Grotto in a letter to Blount, from the same year: "…how little it owes to Art, either the Place itself, or the Image I give of it." Is aware of his initiation into MwOship.

A sigil, a poem with all the words removed. Eventually, he could only stand or sit upright in stays fastened by maid servants.

The motto Pope had inscribed over the entrance to the Grotto—SECRETVM ITER / ET FALLENTIS / SEMITA VITAE, from Horace.—was translated by Abraham Cowley as "The secret tracks of the deceiving life" in his essay "Of Obscurity." I had settled on, A secret journey along the pathway of life.

Pope undertook the Grotto (his self-described "grottofying") on profits from his translation of the *Iliad*. The young poet of "An Essay on Criticism" had written: "Nature and Homer were, he found, the same." And further: "Nature still, but *Nature Methodized*." Kresimir Vukovic points out that Homer's caves are dangerous, not Ovid's spaces of refuge and privacy, where adulteries should be kept secret and out of the daylight. The Dunciad mentions "One cell there is conceal'd from vulgar eye, / The cave of poverty and poetry." But the cave is the province of Dulness. Every civilization builds its inadequate bomb shelter.

Pope's private ferryman Bowry row'd visitors to the Grotto entrance.

Mozart would finish writing "The Magic Flute," according to legend, in a watery cave in the Saltzburg woods.

The translator considers Lackmann, Wolf, and friends of Peisistratus, art reducing Ogilby's oversized page, but in the process emptying Homer's "fire and rapture," offended by language—swearing men, and horny gods. Pope had approved in verse of Gulliver's being used as a dildo; games at Dulness' coronation featured a pissing contest. Isaih submits God's flatulence sounds "like a harp for Moab."

Even the occasional love poem

is restless, unaccustomed to being in bed

beside someone;

the terms of dalliance

a bit too expedient:

"Oh may we never love as these have lov'd!"

His sexually frustrated Belinda

can only hallucinate "bodies chang'd to various forms" in the Cave of Spleen, wherein "Men

prove with child…" The MwO-to become is also an emasculated

man without an organ.

  Recollected in the Dunciad, Dulness' Cave is seen as the womb for the new race of poets:

   "Here she beholds the Chaos dark and deep,

Where nameless somethings in their causes sleep,

'Till genial Jacob, or a warm Third day,

Call forth each mass, a Poem, or a Play:

How hints, like spawn, scarce quick in embryo lie,

How new-born nonsense first is taught to cry,

Maggots, half-form'd in rhyme exactly meet,

And learn to crawl upon poetic feet."

The Grotto of 1739

Christopher Neve writes: "By making perfect geometric constructions, Poussin believes he can not only satisfy the mind but transcend time," *Immortal Thoughts*.

Dorn's Slinger observes: "…we are crystals of gold / along the axes of upheaval." Recalling for me conditions inside the developing MwO, the formations of axes, thresholds, latitudes and longitudes, transitions and becomings.*

> *On becoming: emphasizes the limnal space,
>
> the walk from lawn to garden made ornate
>
> and underfoot, as if interior.

> The masterpiece of Fullness
>
> is Pope's "Epistle to Dr. Arbuthnot,"

"a performance consisting…of many fragments wrought into One design," Samuel Johnson observed. To us, IT IS AN ASSEMBLEAGE, the liberated method of creation that defines activity in the Full. The poem wrote itself in pieces over time ("I lisp'd in Numbers, for the Numbers came"), then finished at great speed as his friend and doctor died. The poem is at turns the kenotic autobiography of the MwO (with Frank O'Hara aplomb) and a satiric fusillade fired his detractors (the ArbuthNOT). From

> I cough like *Horace*, and tho' lean, am short.
>
> *Ammon*'s great Son one shoulder had too high,
>
> Such *Ovid*'s nose, and "Sir, you have an *Eye*——
>
> …
>
> All that disgraced my Betters, met in me."

The letter poem is for another doctor "To help me thro' this long Disease, my Life" with council and friendship

to

Sporus,
Nero's castrato wife, boy victim

to the power
categorization grants,
"breaks a butterfly upon a wheel."
Readers insert
Lord Hervey.

This is the vision of MwO in Fullness.
    Jonathan Richardson's likenesses,
    "Pope in the line of Chaucer"
    and "Pope in the line of Milton,"
score by Handel.
    Pope, Arbuthnot,
    and Humphries
hash'd out Esther, the first English oratorio
"…I obey, To thee I give the day."
    (I confess, I cannot hear Handel, bear
Music with a convenient handle,
Without wishing Messian to be born.
Brendon Urie got the wigs very wrong—
Wigs "helped to delouse the upper class"—
Blake paints Pope "between…the Unfortunate
Lady and Eloisa—and Handel
Is a "manly" presence among the Dunc'd.
Women were bann'd from coffeehouses.)

The Grotto of 1744

Pope in the Cancer stage
                              attempted a restart,
            a reset to Fullness,
plenum only succeeded in adding
kitsch to the Grotto.
Groundskeeper John Searle describes
the contents of one room,
"as it was left after {Pope's} death":

Several large Pieces of fine Crystal intermix'd with Yellow Mundie; a fine Piece of Spar interwoven like many Oyster-shells, and intermix'd with White Mundie; a fine Piece of Spar with a Mixture of Copper interwoven like a fine Lace; several Pieces of Crystal with brown Incrustation and a Mixture of Mundic, from the Hertz Mines in Germany; a fine Piece of Gold Ore from the Peruvian Mines; Silver Ore from the Mines of Mexico; several Pieces of Silver Ore from Old Spain; some large Pieces of Gold Clift, from Mr. Cambridge in Gloucestershire. Lead Ore, Copper Ore, white Spar, petrified Wood, Brazil Pebbles, Egyptian Pebbles and Blood-stones, from Mr. Brinsden. Some large Clumps of Amethyst, and several Pieces of White Spar, from the Duchess of Cleveland. Some fine Pieces of Red Spar, several fine Isicles, and several sorts of Fossils, from George Littleton, Esq; Many Pieces of Coral and petrified Moss, and many other curious Stones from the Island of St. Christopher in the West Indies; with several Humming Birds in their Nests, from Anthony Brown, Esq; of Abbs-Court in Surrey. Plymouth Marble of different Colours, one fine Cornish Diamond from the Prince's Mine in Cornwall, near a Hundred Weight, from the Reverend Dr. Askew. Several fine Pieces of Yellow Mundic; some Purple Copper stained by Mineral Water; two Stones from the Giants Causeway in Ireland, from Sir Hans Sloan; some Pieces of petrified Wood, with Coral and petrified Moss round a Bason of Water.

Reads like "A City Shower," Swift's decriptio.

Pope's "Verses on a Grotto…,"1741/1743:

Thou who shalt stop, where *Thames'* translucent Wave

Shines a broad Mirrour thro' the shadowy Cave;

Where lingering Drops from Mineral Roofs distill,

And pointed Crystals break the sparkling Rill,

Unpolish'd Gemms no Ray on Pride bestow,

And latent Metals innocently glow:

Approach Great NATURE studiously behold!

And eye the Mine without a Wish for Gold.

Approach: But awful! Lo th' *AEgerian* Grott,

Where, nobly-pensivee ST. JOHN sate and thought;

Where *British* Sighs from dying WYNDHAM stole,

And the bright Flame was shot thro' MARCHMONT'S Soul.

Who dare to love their Country, and be poor.

  Pope elaborates wildly like cells multiplying, barely organized, in this Cancerous stage MwO. Here, Wyndham and Marchmont appear among the philosophers, sponsored by reading (Livy's Cave); Egeria is Pope's muse.

Our MwO has grown beyond classifications but is lost without immediately forging new ones. Johnson says, in his Life of Pope: "…excavation was requisite as an entrance to his garden, and, as some men try to be proud of their DEFECTS, he extracted an ornament from an inconvenience, and vanity produced a grotto where necessity enforced a passage." (Emphasis is mine.)

"I plant, root up, I build, and then confound, / Turn round to square, and square again to round," Epistle to Bolingbroke.

Hurriedly Revised Thesis:

The MwO in his Cancerous stage attempts a restart

left unfinished at death,

his most incoherent work, a satire of satires,

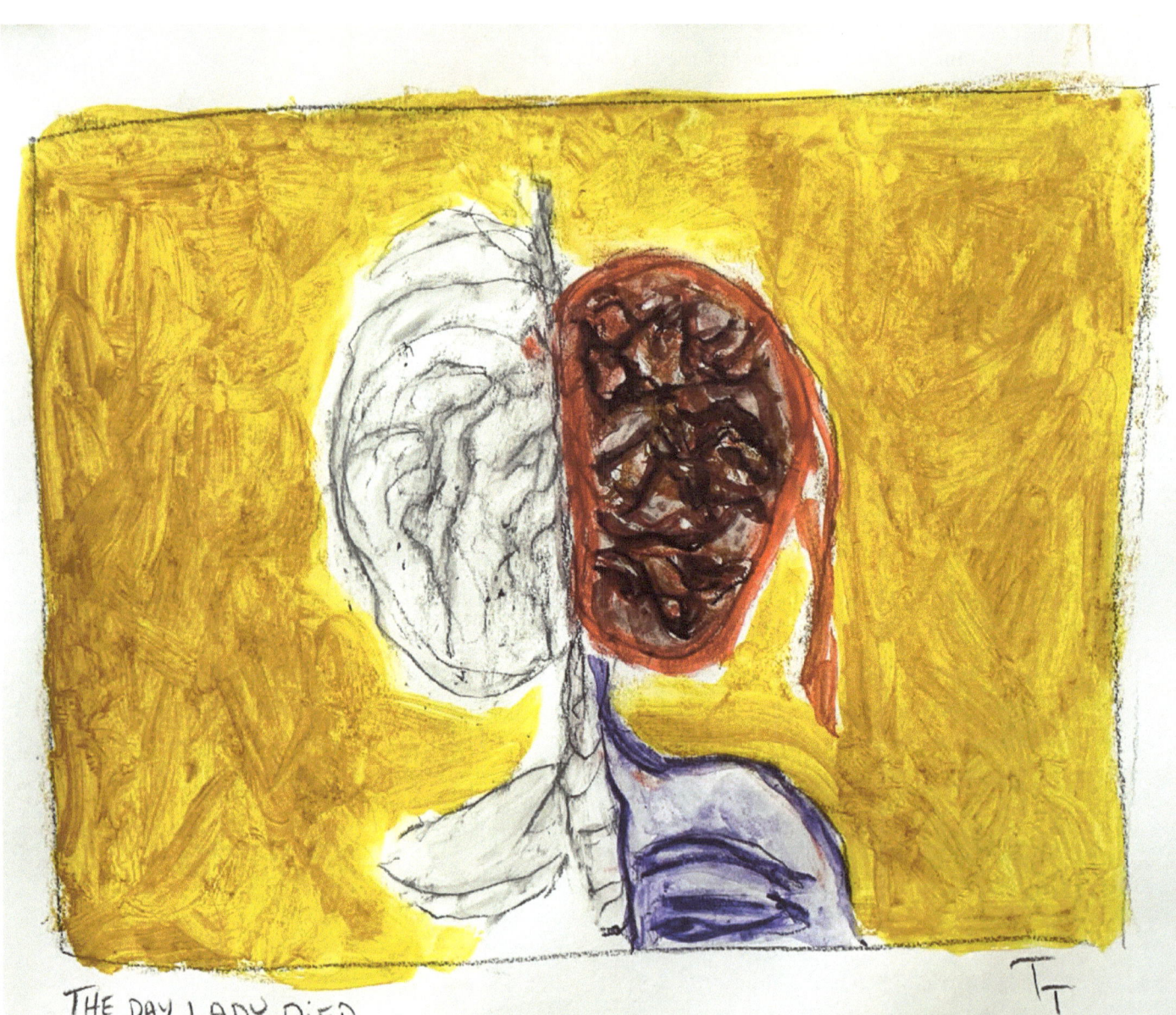

THE DAY LADY DIED

not possible again until Duchamp's "Given States."
The cotton cloud behind the mannequin as poor
Quality as the Preservation Trust's animated digital reconstruction of Pope's
riverview from the Grotto, obscured only by the willow tree he planted.
When he no longer wrote,
objects appearing in dreams
began to collect in the Grotto.
The tunnel's spring is long dried up.
Low rooms of rimeless puns,
the last puns from the avowed hater of puns,
overrun with tours and scholars—

    "Shut, shut the door, good John!...
    Tie up the knocker, say I'm sick, I'm dead.'"

Land's countdown reaches zero.

Boulder

Dear Ed,

Most of the people left in the world who can read Pope for pleasure were gathered before me to listen. What could I say, in the end? Something about Anti-Oedipus. You would know what to say. Your own critique of money is flawless.

For weeks, everything reminded me of Pope, now there is the ride to the airport and the long flight back: the Grotto tube empties out into the Boeing tube with the force of bigger through smaller Reagan will still be president at home. The Great Communicator of the "uncreating word." Did you get to London? I'm sorry we didn't connect after all.

Enclosed is a pamphlet from the occasion.

You have to bow your head to enter the Grotto, remove your hat, like the set up for Napoleon but without the body.

Love

P/S Are you still mad abt my Tom Clarke review?

Home, I see Kitaj's collage "His Every Poor, Defeated, Loser's, Hopeless Move, Loser Buried (Ed Dorn)" looks like somebody's walking fast past the Grotto.

APPENDIX

(Including Notes Variorum,
Remarks, Abhorences, Imitations, & Corrections,
As in the Fourth Dunciad)

"POPE TURNED THE tongue of A Literature"

Don't Start with the Shard

Pope materializ'd on Barbicon
Looking for Grub Street, his hysterical
Speeches sounding like Artaud translat'd.
Give me your hand, I own your opinions.
Try nothing before you sit him down in
Twickenham, within the restor'd Grotto.
The city is as new as his to me.

The Curliad
Edmund Curll imitation

The only time we met, De Form'd stands me
A Drink he doctors when my back is turn'd.

So it was I came to publish that night
Volumes of Vomitus under his name.

Pirate! Plagiarist! Pornographer!
And they pillori'd me in his name.

I've heard the prince of Ipicac
Carried Pistols when he walked the dog,

Be that so, who carried Him, if not
Cibber-like his tireless Hypercritics?

Vanity's Visionary! Despot by Personification!
Even Broome was not immune to trashing.

"A strong Vomit would kill me," admitt'd
The shifty little Shit to Doctor Swift.

Pope promised, There will always be Wars
And rumors of Workshops. He fir'd the first

Name in vain at Iowa, inspir'd
The revolt that claims Infighting

Is poetry. The Naropa workshop
Lost everything when his Theobald

Sets fire to the cornfield, burns everything
Save for Mary Toft's Scriblerian brood.

De Form'd as Poet's overwhelmingly
Formful, Hogarthian mincing martyr

To Inherited belief, yea, the Child
Of Belief beside herself—Pope's Progress.

Bewigg'd explorer into finite Multiplicity
In his brick basement, forgot to consult

The Genius of the Place about the Cave.
(Double check the deed: Pope has reopen'd

Baldo's Cave of Fools next door to you.)
Hatred's self-anointed Hater.

Most social of horrors. The Outsid'r
Records insid'r Gossip, Pope's dope.

The five-foot Hogarth sketch'd a humpback Pope,
With Kent and those tasteless Polladians.

Fresh libels maintain fashion and jurists
In wigs. Heaping new stones on old
Satiates neither Cave nor appetite.

Why Hogarth saw "The Distrest Poet"
And not landowner in the Dunciad.

That's Pope handing down to us his latest
Construction "The Sleeping Congregation,"

For we only have Eyes
    For the well-turned Mistress.

Richard Bentley Imitation

You are not man enough to wipe the snot,
Sir, from Arbuthnot's nose, a pinch of snuf
And off you fly, amusing irritant,
A bad habit dispell'd into the air,
Our most quot'd and seldom read poet.
Perhaps you know his "Esssay Concerning
The Effects of Air on Human Bodies"
("A tame Bird cannot fly so well," he wrote,
"As a wild one."), or is your preferr'd text
The prose History of John Bull, perchance?
You were never as clear as your doctor.
You needn't ask permission to libel
Me in the pretentious obscenity
"Sober Advice from Horace." I *do* ask
"Why Imitated? Why not translated?"
You might have taken physician' advice
And waited another nine years to print.
One's self-taught Latin should be kept at home.
The best that can be said for you is just
False Praise: QUI NIL MOLITUR INEPTE.

The Stuff'd Owl
Colley Cibber Imitation

No tour is complete without dropping by
The Grotto & Gift Shop's newest room,

Fool's Gold, gift from the gifted Arch Hades.
If the lines are intolerably long,

One might opt for the color Postcyard
And a signed copy of Arcadia.

Think complete no reading of his Work
Without My tale of Pope at the Brothel.

Coffee before Tea
Dudley Ryder Imitation

For my Penny, I get coffee and Talk;
Song lasting as long as I can listen.
I pays my money and I sit smoking,
Never dare to submit my epistle
Through the ivory Gate Hogarth design'd
To resemble a mailbox on a Door.
I sneak home whistling a morning air,
A stain'd great Coat reeking smoke and Poems.

"WHAT fuck order'd the espresso TO GO?"

TT

40

It Flows from Here
Abhorrence

Coffee house Starbucks bann'd I phone handguns

Double espresso with sugar lyric

Piping hot at their regular table

Tall no-foam latte is the critic's choice

Lingering, a bit too esoteric

Feeling talkative? dark bean in a mug

A pot of caffeine would write a memoir

Talking about poems is a lost art

Any poem in any century

What fuck order'd the espresso TO GO?

Pope's footnote for John Dennis

Now I will criticize the Critics,

Those *heavy Mules…neither Horse or Ass,*

Who judge poetry and religion a fit.

(*So vast is Art, so narrow Human Wit.*)

A Good Verse must first be a Tool

For sanctioned Passion that elevates Fools,

Teaches the creator of Stage Thunder.

History replac'd him with Oldmixor.

Epistle for Nomi

Pope went to Temple to "see for himself"
The ruling passion van Loo glimps'd
Only to find, abandon'd there, himself.
Exemplar character is splendorous
Curl'd up at home for another lap nap;
The childless mother's tolerance, briefly
Relax'd curiosity, sees in dark;
You exude the comfort no one gave you.
(Cibber power naps in the goddess' lap,
Fake snooze. Dulness makes "a poet's form" walk
A de-form'd visitor's sad defective
Manner of walking-by-counting off steps
To the retreat in manor room mirrors.
Vico's barbarism of reflection.)
Cobham walk'd away from complicity.
Installing him in the academy
Is the end of Pope, best left wandering
The grounds with friends, burying enemies;
Sleepless in the palace at 4 AM.
Disturbing his many selves taking notes
For the Variorum, disquiet'd
At the first modern longpoem crowning.

"Present in the poem" is a problematic notion, for it is not easy to decide what or where "the poem" is…very difficult in fact to draw the poem's boundaries, to decide what is "in" it, what is not in it, where poem leaves off and biography begins.—Griffin, p. 219, on the Dunciad & variorum.

If he thought of something in the midst of the night, he rang for the servant to bring paper; if something struck him during a conversation, he would immediately write it down for further use.—Auden.

You are too difficult to be around.
Is tomorrow a good time to visit?

Work Without Hope

My Contract with Dust stipulates the terms.
You sign your signature in the wrong hand
So authenticity, as an autograph's,
Becomes a question of your word or hers.
The great advantage was knowing his life
Would be over before his enemies',
So he felt Free to memorialize.
Give me your Hand, I own your opinions.
We'll make a brilliant controversy.

The Hack

I saw at once something I could be not
Olson's poet of verse/reverse—Adverse.
I'm a Grub Street hack, Tobias Smollett.
We need no cemetery on Grub Street,
Just a coffeehouse stool for a desk.
Artaud and Genet took rooms on Grub Street.
That line about Querelle being 'a boy
Whose soul had changed into an alligator,'
I'll steal, the day Grub turns into Milton,
In the manner of Roderick Random,
Equally at home at sea and Grub Street,
Where everyone's a shady character.
If you are Peter Gordon, then fuck you.

Epistle to Bertholf

Spent my sabbatical becoming Pope.
Recherche cloak'd in black within the Grotto
Like a spider, splay'd legs and arms, no sense
Of time, reading by candlelight only.
Quills carefully sharpen'd for the ink well.
I'm at the Coffee House
I'm at the bookstore
I'm at the combination starbucks and barnes & noble
I don't like their knock-off drinks, I don't read
books like that, the outlets for my laptop

Are taken. So I read Paris Review
For the interviews without buying it.
Once in a while, when you weren't looking,
Your fierce love of Wallace Stevens flar'd up
Like an old hockey injury. I nod.
In dreams, Bertholf is always brilliant
Gossiping about Duncan's trogs, about
Who they were. "No Follower, but a Friend."
Hone no more subscribes to a Scriblerian
Lineage than Black Mountain. After Olson
There enters Tom Clark, a lark following
Geography; soon there came John Sheffield
And his circle, introducing Anne Finch.
If there's a breach, "The lock won't cost the head."

Dorn might bring to class (this was Lit Am West)
The Landlock'd in Kent, to keep us up; to turn us on
The physician poet is nam'd Gael Turnbull!
Names as obscure to me as Keats and Yeeets.
"Nevertheless, it is dangerous to be named and makes you mortal."
He was two years out of Davies' Essex,
CO is less than three years dead. The tape
He play'd of the reading at Berkeley
Would take me the next five years to unwind.
The first two books of *Gunslinger* in print.
Elaine Feinstein had receiv'd that Letter
Before Ed join'd her on the faculty.
Pope with his fast friend Whitson must have seen
The eclipse of 4/22/15
As part of what Gay call'd Pope's involvement

In "the revolution of eclipses."
Sinclair records Dorn and Prynne were eager
To view the solar eclipse at Cornwall,
Ed's "big event," or the Millenium.

Mock Epic

The victim's cutting herself to pieces
Fit for trash bags was rul'd a suicide.
Meanwhile, the murderer remains at large;
Pope knows Cibber is his poem's hero.
The poet's testimony under oath,
Shot full of one hole by the gazetteers,
Should be requir'd reading at Cam and Isis,
Whose tenur'd assholes resurrect the Classics,
But "murder first, and mince them all to bits."
(Are you trying to describe Dorn, Slinger?)

This Time Reading Ed's "Derelict Airs"
When I aim at praise, they say I bite.

His weakness was intelligence soaring
Above allegiances to kings and church.

Snuf debates Taste in our age, banners clash:
Did he drink Coke or Pepsi? The poet

Outwits himself, plants minefields of footnotes
That hobble readers too few for armies.

New Epistle to Burlington, from L. George

After 200 years, David Smith's *Letter*
Has arriv'd at the spirit of the place.
You can read the old sky and water page
Between the lines from your daughters' missive:
O   WHY   O
WHY   DID   I
EVER   LEAVE
O   HI   O?

When I am Pope, I know the Day of my Death

The total Eclipse of the sun, fathers
Fear'd the world's end, become a bidness Boon.
Langland monks are renting out their cells
To solar watchers, the Tower is book'd.
'Twas Belinda's "eyes that must eclipse the day,"
So areolas occlude the rake's sight
Momentarily between light and light.
The Trojan horse blames the dons, half consum'd
"My head has gone to college for a year,"
The Butt complains in Duncan's lampoon,
"And I have nothing but my backsides left."
Ceaselessly chewing stacks of meatless bones.
Tibbald is "darkness visible"
Opening the seals, Walpole ascending.
Halley predict'd the Totality
Alas, Pope can only muster frozen
Dinners for the return of Burlington.
Birds fall speechless, stars emerge in the Dark,
Halys ends the war in a draw;
Then Eclipse, "uncreating word," is gone.

    I think I've seen all this before, the stars
Are always waiting behind the curtains,
It hasn't been so long since Villiers'
Rehearsal made the sun, the moon, earth dance;
Lacy's delivery in Dryden's tone
Hilarious before Cibber fuck'd it.
Why is it so easy to change the date,
Picture Walpole in a cart in Scotland

Cheating at scores, chasing a little ball?
It shouldn't be easy. Next, parliament
Chang'd the date of Halley's Eclipse, April,
Dropping 11 days from the calendar.
London's 213 seconds marks
The dusk that is our Darkness

[Gregorian May 3rd 1715, or Today, April 8th 2024]

Footnote

We had imagined this twilight as something like a sunset…
We failed to imagine how ghostly an evening without sunset would be.
—Stifter, "The Solar Eclipse of July 8th, 1842."

Vowels
Footnote

"Like friendly colours found them both unite,
And each for each contract new strength and light."
Fulgent mornings in Jervis' studio
Drawing only to throw away drawings.
(Milton creat'd his style translating
From Greek into English and back again.)
He digests the portrait painter's lessons
Like Mummimus' treasure after years
And deliver'd Homeros in COLOR.
"Thou but preserv'st a Face and I a Name."

Trogs & Dunces
Footnote

Troglodytes the term originally
Meant reactionary dwellers in Caves.
Who calls Peirce, follow'r of Duns Scotus,
A "dunce," tho' he design'd his house beside
A River that since mov'd itself away?
Pope won't leave Diaper holding his breath
In the weeds, moving from lawn to water.

SYLLABUS FOR A COURSE ON BATHOS

Alexander Pope, *Alcander, Prince of Rhodes*, 1704.

——————-, *Peri Bathous, Or the Art of Sinking in Poetry*, 1728.

Richard Blackmore, *Prince Arthur, an Heroick Poem in Ten Books*, 1695.

——————, *King Arthur, an Heroic Poem in Ten Books*, 1697.

——————-, *Elize, an Epik Poem in Ten Books*, 1705.

——————-, *Creation, a Philosophical Poem in Seven Books*, 1712.

——————-, *Redemption, a Divine Poem in Six Books*, 1722.

——————, *Alfred, an Epik Poem in Twelve Books*, 1723.

> "Sick was the sun,… /
> Then rose the seed of Chaos, and of Night,
> To blot out order, and extinguish light….
Dulness decrees that epic poetry
Won't be written in the age of commerce:
> 'Be sure I give them fragments, not a meal.'"

"The internet is the Dunciad," Tod.

They bust'd Agon Schiele for painting
Desire-machines; so he sketch'd his lock'd door.

Wheaton Out

My copy of Mack's Life was discard'd
By the renovat'd Wheaton Public:
Three slender biographies take precious space,
Three adjuncts for the price of one tenure,
Free up the size of Little Popcorn Store
Til phones eliminate brick and mortar.
This used book has a history. I see
John Belushi still owes a late fee—
Toothless Bobby Hull holds it up and grins
50 times for the cameras—
Folks came to the old library to look
Hoping to catch Red Grange reading the book.

Epistle by Denny Lyons, Day 51.

I went to bed sick, glad to surrender
My broken string of a poem a day.

Lucky me, this season walks count as hits.
I wake, a center field sun thrills my eyes,

The feeder attracting consecutive birds
Like poems with big appetites for playing.

Warburton Changed Pope's Dialogue to Epistle
Footnote

I wish Alice Notley would contact Pope
For me, before I realize I have
Already done that, writing this poem.

"I hear the dead speaking" sounds very Jones.
Speak in tongues, Jack Spicer, being cautious
To wake yourself before you handle snakes.

The trance of reading Pope releases me,
At the introduction of his own footnotes,
To a tree full of angels, Blake might pause
Work to welcome Milton into the room.
Only the sitter sees and hears Blake talk:

Jones Very is what the second coming look'd like—
Ed Dorn is how the second Pope sounds.

The BwO Books An Appearance
He hangs between.

Our ventriloquist drinks off the water
He'd made a show of pouring with steady hands
To show his poem is on the level
And originating outside himself.
Note the artist research'd every detail

Creating a puppet that looks like Pope.
Now smoking a weed, he recites Cibber:
"'Til Wisdom can make me more heartily
Happy, I am content to be GAZED at.'"*
Follow'd by Applause. Bows. Flagging hand claps.
The dummy, collaps'd on the vacant stool,
Keeps delivering punch lines in the dark.
This speaking from the gut seems virtuous
Like my intentional catachresis;
His voice in my head sounds familiar—
Dummy is a body without organs.

*Pope "quotes" Cibber in *Peri Bathous.*

Roc Marie

Pope knows nothing about love that Ovid
And Bononcini didn't. The body
Without organs is a break in the flow
Of that continuity connecting
Anonymous lovers. Pope himself might
Be kept alive on machines or unplugg'd.
It should have been enough to understand,
The pinch of snuf Robert Jaulin gave Pope
Originat'd from a single leaf
Extending as far as the universe.
But Twickenham was built on many spines.
The cottage on Roc Marie has hous'd

Decades of love poetry, dating
From Ed Dorn's Songs for the newly married.
Once, I was invit'd in for coffee,
Conversation, and birdsong, when I gleen'd
Pope's "Nature Methodiz'd" means Pat and Dean's
Ohio gardening, not just Homer.

AP Plants a Tree

It never does for long for a finger
To hold one's place in volumes; long fingers
Will soon be call'd to handier matters,
The coffee is made, and the place is lost,
Page where the letter-press finger points.
Laying the book face down will break the spine;
The dog-ear'd page is an ear with no -ring.
Where are all those bookmarks friends gave one,
Years of ribbons misquoting Dickinson?
Someone who open'd this book when it was New
Has press'd iniside twigs off weeping willow,
Long ago fus'd into the yellow page.

[Young Pope contribution to Garth's Ovid
was The Fable of Dryope become a tree.]

This May 4

Spider can feel fire now so pulls its legs
Into his ink body, the period
At the end of a sentence. Library
Is the biggest fire, making hideous
Faces in the crowd as they warm one side.
I myself threw bags of syllables more
Or less than 10 into the Inferno.

Visitation on Water Street

At my whistle, appreciatory
Epistle for that line in the Turbine
Dorn's great white dog of place appears wanting
Food. I may not know dogs but I can see
This one is starving. Benefactor lost,
He sleeps in libraries and night classes,
Makes the rounds selling stolen books of hair.
The great white dog of place manag'd to sniff
Out the line from the Black Sea to London
To Kent by Lawrence. (My conspiracy
Thesis is, he got pack'd with the boxes.)
He shall consume everything in his path.
Kimball is a composite pack'd from two
Grad students wagging a single tail.
To this day, a gathering of poets
Greater than three is known as a bertholf.

Footnote for Brutus at Troy

Pope compos'd pages a day, every day,
Taking time out to teach Homer English,
See doctors, or correct Shakespeare's meter.
He was already writing Choruses
In blank verse for the epic Brutus.
No, there is no "poetry of old age."
You write as long and as far as you can;
Then write beyond the end of Critics' cant.
Ruffhead reads Pope's extensive Plans,
Deliberate as Bellot's Dialogues,
Three long prose columns to every page.
Blazek and Yeats undertake, in old age,
Revisions to their posterior work;
Others will hire new crews, buy insurance,
Rope, canvas, caulk, and paint for the voyage.
Pope wore three pairs of stockings so his calves
Look'd bigger below a face made for busts;
Silk padding seldom made the weak line fine.
  "At length [Brutus] resolves to go in a single ship,
    and to reject all as dared not accompany him."
No need for remodel, spontaneous
The couplet on Bounce's death arriv'd last.

Pope Always Named His Dogs Bounce

Did this Bounce enjoy the run of the house?
Perhaps a more formal relationship
Necessitating lessons and restraint,
As Art domesticates higher Nature,
An ornate frame improves the picture.
Did she love to lap the lawn, lost and found
In the Grotto after an all-hands search?
Did Pope call a servant to fetch her
From a succession of Bounces, painted
First by Richardson to Great Dane guard dogs
Then, in between the times, Bounce to Swift's Fop?
Did the ghosts of all Pope's dogs come running
Every time he invok'd the good name Bounce?
She reclines into the sofa, becomes
Her luxuriant fur entanglements,
Combs out gentlemen's talk from doggy dreams.
The many Homers are now orthodox;
We call four Dunciads the Dunciad;
All the selves over a lifetime, myself.
Stein's repetitive naming all her dogs
Basket drove Picasso nuts when he came
To paint her portrait he couldn't settle
On one head to sit atop the owner.

On the Efficacy of Naming All Kings "Charles"

Pope roll'd wrong. The Revolt against Dulness
Fail'd because we let Her live, rent free, in-
Side the body without organs of TWO
Future kings of the dope show nam'd CHARLES.
Wrong to believe de Form could be royal.
Altho' Walpole subscrib'd to Pope's Odyssey,
Abhorrence is the national epic.

The Epistle to Augustus
Horace Imitation

The road to Pope is never straight ahead.
He inverts Horace's praise to Caesar
To egg the edifice George Augustus
then merrily drives off into prank night
Assur'd the king can't call the cops on him
And acknowledge His faults for the insults:
Because guilt provides context for satire.
Yet people read it straight, no inside quotes.
Ribald Pope jok'd Eggs with Lady Mary
In the bad taste Capon's Tale revision.
Even Taylor quoting out of context
"The sound must seem an echo to the sense"
Misses out on the cosmic connection.
Pope is the great contextualizer
In English literature. And then Pound.

"Pete + REPEAT my mother CALL'D ALL HER SONS"

TT

Ovid did for the pagan world. Dante's
Beatrice bespoke Milton's latinate Eve.
Byron's hero mocks Pope; Dorn does Olson.
Olson's student call'd the Reformation
"Late Greek authoritarianism."
All my asides act to provide contexts
(Maximus is all context no poem).
"'Let me be Horace, and be Ovid you.'"
Better, let me be Tibullus, sad heart
Of a man, and you can bemoan me in
An elegy for all my elegies,
"Weave Laurel Crowns, and take what Names we please."
Pete and Repeat my mother call'd her sons,
Pretext and sub.

Pope Emeritus
Abhorrence

Mr. Lee Van Cleef, please inform Ed Dorn
For me, he indeed Conforms afterall.
We've talli'd the last absentee ballot—
And you're in! All late congratulations.
The position works something like tenure
To enure poetry against judgments
That obscure the history of the place.
You're only requir'd to be a genius.
You won't have an office in the building.
    And then round up Pope, warn him

A new kid is gunning for him. Best build
Two coffins. Hammer, if you will, softly.
This department ain't big enuf for both
Of them, this parallel moment of truth.

The Carcass

1. No meat was served at Pope's table, for he hated the butchery of animals.

2. Quennell, a poor judge of Pope's person, has Johnson swear otherwise:
"…he loved meat highly seasoned and of strong taste," a dying man seeking
pleasure.

3. Great Danes such as Bounce were bred for hunting, an irony that could not
have been wasted on Pope.

4. The gourmet vegetarian, Auden reminds us, Pope "cooked his correspondence."

5. The poet of "An Essay on Man" pictures the lamb who "licks the hand just raised to shed his
blood."

6. As a boy, he was trampled by a cow and nearly killed.
      I blank out, in the shadow of the cow
      Going wild over me, this must be death.

7. Pope starts up his essay for *The Guardian* with Pilpai's fable of the fated Cow, and describes
an English kitchen looking like "a giant's den in a romance, bestrewed with scattered heads
and mangled limbs" ("Against Barbarity to Animals," May 1713).

8. Dinner guests arrive by barge and enter
Thro' the Grotto. Hunters were invit'd
To eat their own words, under the table
With the dogs. His publishers brot their own
Knives and sporks. Thro'out, the little host's toes
Were never once observ'd to touch the floor.

9. Pope called his body "the Carcase."

"John Dryden Meeting with Alexander Pope"
A Note

The old engraving is unconvincing,
The scene too cleverly theatrical:

Stage right, a chair left overturned; at left,
Some gentleman pours wine into a glass,

No one else is drinking, everyone sports
Elaborate wigs but poet and kid.

"Who are all these people and doing what?"
Actors pack the room where Dryden, who should be

Bedridden succumbing to poverty,
Sits grumpy in the only other chair,

More posing than receiving, and laying
Laureate hands on the boy a la Mode,

Who had yet to go up to the city
Or even read Dryden's Fables, he should

Be in the year tuberculosis bent
The bow of his spine. "Who is this cripple

They want me to heal?" the old man wonders
If he might outlive the younger poet.

The sources perpetuate myth-making.
Both poets claimed they met but didn't.

"[H]e persuaded some friends, to take him
To the coffeehouse Dryden frequented,

And pleased himself with having seen him."
Pope lied about his age for Johnson's Life.*

*See L.V. Mountweazel, "Plasmic Echo."
All this for want of a cell-phone selfie.

Merch from the Cash Site
Abhorrence

We live in the aftermath of a Crash

And something's missing. Investigating

Armies thinking to gather the limbs have

Assembl'd Osiris without a Cock.

Reconstruction is futile: Dunciad

Can never happen again. Among us,

Maybe Fassbinder knew such readiness.

There are no survivors and Pope left us

The flight Manifesto but no idea

How the protract'd thing flew across water.

His is not first if there is no second.

The pieces are reconstruct'd across

The concrete floor in the form of a jet.

(Tourist editors lur'd to the Grotto

Holding tickets for the Restoration

And their breath.) In the day, all these names

Were human flesh hanging from trees made flesh.

Kristi writes her special place in the Noem,

Who shot the open face of poesy

For disobeying rules of prosody.

Cosmic Toryism
Abhorrence

"Awake, my St. John," you've slept thro' thunder
Dreaming that rain drops bounce like mercury.
Whatever is, is not good enough good;
And everything is not for a reason.
Tebeaux's Pope writes "Essay on Man" because
"All metaphysics are inadequate."
Voltaire translates Bolingbroke's epistle—
Rousseau writes Voltaire it taught him "patience"—
Kant believes Pope was a philosopher
More profound than Leibniz. Then they recant.
Now, the biography of the poem
Includes Willey's "cosmic Toryism."
The dead worm in Artaud's brain, I remain,
"Bewilder'd in the Maze of Scholars."

It's Your Birthday, And You Give Me A Gift
(or, On Receiving Dean Keller's Books of AP's Translations)

Nobody read Chapman much anymore,*
Their Homer sang English in Pope's clear Voice:
"Be Homer's Works your study and Delight,
Read them by Day, and meditate by Night."**
Def host was showing off his folio,
Dangling the Epic like an antique
For poor Keats who, like ignorant Cortez,
Arriv'd at the wrong place at the right time.

Even then, it was chance not choice trapp'd Keats
Chastely "looking into" Antiquity,
Alternating with Clarke they rapp'd all night,***
Dancing home crunk at 6, chune in his head
Messag'd back to Clarke, record'd by dawn.
There was no time for Immortality.

*One American reader, Herman Melville, so preferred Chapman's Homer that he carried it around Cape Horn. But Poe indicates, in a letter to Judge Tucker, his study of scansion in Pope's work. Po(p)e. Abigail Adams was fond of quoting Pope in her letters. The wait, from Walpole placing his pocket Pope Iliad on display in his Strawberry Hill library, is until Vendler for Pope to be a poet thinking, producing the verse essay. Samuel Johnson established early on the critical line on Pope's Homer: "His version may be said to have turned the English tongue; for since its appearance no writer, however deficient in other powers, has wanted melody." If Ovid in exile wrote in a new tongue, then Pope turned the tongue of a literature.
**Among contemporary detractors, his offense was Pope's Homer "does not talk like Homer"
    Because he could not bear Homer's bat-like
    Souls of Men, he dropt the offending lines.
Later, Novalis said that speech is translation.
***"Rap Madrigal" from An Essay on Man
What woeful stuff this madrigal would be,
In some stary'd hackney sonneteer, or me?
But let a Lord once own the happy lines,
How the wit brightens! how the style refines!

Correction

Novalis, a mining engineer, knew
Minerals and grottoes, not habitats.

The Pope Sessions
Remarks

My concession is typing to Glenn Gould
Playing daily over the last three months
Attending the Pope sessions, production
Set for his birthday on the 21st,
Expecting to be replac'd by AI
Nevertheless faithful in my prime seat.
Gould practis'd on piano Handel's four
Suites and recor'd on the harpsicord;
Sav'd the idiosyncrasies for Bach,
As if Handel prepar'd Art of the Feud.
He ate the score and made it new for me.

II

Let's agree to pretend Rape of the Lock
Exists as a lost works title
Instead of the insufferably long
Conurbation we must daily commute
Since London mov'd away the countryside.
Good. We know Pope as the perpetrator
Of Dunciad, builder of the Grotto.

(Maybe even working on the poem
From underground)…Trying to get this far
Conjures up the image of the writer's
Mighty struggle with his diseas'd Prostrate
To pee a drop atop flaming critics.

III

I want'd to add something about how
The aesthetic is at heart musical,
His meditations work like scores Wallace
Stevens heard as Auroras of Autumn.
His aphorisms look easy as rime,
The inevitable answer to what
Comes next. PICTURE FRANK O'HARA AND POPE.
Choosing life in an unheat'd villa
Requires patience to wait for sun to warm.
He was sun-center in a coterie;
Became the dog star ante O'Hara.
PICTURE FRANK O'HARA TALKING TO POPE.
Lady Day has been the big surprise!

IV

Pope was a social man, you can see it
In his letters, forev'r battling
Distance & Disease to visit and rec've
Legion Friends, always in their service.

Live Pope

Abhorrence

If you call the dog / you get the dog.

NOT AGAIN! Alexander Pope has been
Way too many times Jimmy Kimmel's guest
Over the last three months, a regular.
It's bad, I can't doze off before midnight.
The TV has to be on and tun'd in.
He's promoting the pre-publication
Of Dunciad IV, announcing his plans
For a vegetarian cooking show.
His accent is funnier than Jimmy's;
He comes across a bit like Gore Vidal,
If you go back that far. Who won the war?
Just ask about the royal family
And let him go. Other topics: culture,
Taste, books, science and religion, gardens.
Bring back Ben Afflick Danny DeVito
Paris Hilton Whoopi Goldberg Judd Hirsch
Magic Johnson Kris Lemche Seal
Chris Pine (did I say Michael Keaton yet?)
Nicholas Cage Eminem—or Ringo.
Bring back from the dead Helen Vendler's smile-
Before-pouncing on the mouse she's caught.
I want to hear Theda Bara talk trash,
Her eyes below du Barry wigs flashing.
The French word "chair" translates into our *flesh*;
Pope's joke makes a table of chair-eaters!
Gasp Quick take Applause Cut to commercial

For my brother Mark

Stood on Its End
Footnote

Dulness has her way: all institutions
Not Her are duly gutt'd and shutter'd.
At he risk of his most scandalous note,
Pope ends his Book with a yawn and a speech

Interrupt'd by the Ten askerisks,
Scannable Line without Organs!

*   *   *   *   *   *   *   *   *   *

Encript'd Sonnet

Very will'd him(self) to become a Man
Without will, surrender'd his Self to God.
Believ'd the Sonnet is sufficient Form;
Went mad as Artaud over BwO.
When very is an adverb, beyond noun,
Assuming at last the eternal life
Where Enoch will shake hands with Emerson.

The Supplicant

Very came down to Harvard ambitious
To "restore the epic." They haul'd him off
To write a howl of sonnets from McLean
After divinity school came to him
The century before Caligula's
Hospital workshop for Sexton and Plath.
Lowell discover'd free verse on the Coast.
In the "Shakespeare" essay, Very conceiv'd
Of the Bard as an open poet
Whose instinct has overcome the structures.
Very's Shakespeare prophesi'd Edward Dorn.

AI Poem

I made a folio and wrote this down.
Having once lived in the world amidst men
And things, the words came rushing back again.
While walking with Alcott, I learned to use
His feet instead of my own. My voice-made-
Hollow echoed his. I could have been John
The Baptist. My body was another's.
In pictures, the saints exhibit symptoms
Of developmental ADHD.

Kenosha Kenosis

Very, in conversation with Channing,
Walked to the fire and, "In obedience
To the Spirit," placed his arm on the mantel.
(J.F. Clarke, "Biographical Notice")

I am the poet's ghost writer
Now pagan, now Whig.
My poems are documentaries.
I write Like New poems
In the form of imbrications.
I have no will of my own.
No organs.
I will inhabit your voice at a cost.
The hubris of the ghostwriter is not
More seemly.
I have gutted the organs of the god
Who ordered angels around him to sing
Unending couplets of orthodoxy
Making eternity sound redundant;
All together—BEAT THOSE PALMS WITH YOUR TONGUES!
Follow Vachel the choirmaster's waving signs in the air!
BLEAT!
Enunciate the Greek phonetically.

A Chronology

1738

Pope was 50 this year and done with Horatian satires.
He corresponds briefly with Aaron Hill.

1838

This September, at Harvard, tutor Very tells the students
in his Greek class: "Flee to the mountains! The end of time
is near!"

1938

Artaud's collection of essays is published as The Theatre
and Its Double.

1948

January 16—French national radio recording session for
"Theatre of Cruelty" includes sound effects for "judgment
of god."
February 1—French Radio censors "judgement of god"
the day before its scheduled broadcast.
March 4—Antonin Artaud dies, at 51.

2021

"1738" (slang), verb meaning to drink Cognac. Coined by Milan Modi for Fetty Wap.

"Musaeus"
Footnote

William Mason's drawing "A Monody"
Puts the poet dying in his Grotto
Attend'd by a mourning Thalia
Witness'd by three male figures (suggesting
Milton, Shakespeare, and Chaucer left to right?
Not Dante, who mock'd the pastoral Muse
And assign'd Thalia to Comedy).
Then where's Dryden? Was Homer invit'd?

Pope's Puppies

To say Emerson outliv'd Jones Very
Is just a sentence. We are sorry But
This isn't what we're looking for at present.
You have plenty of unresolv'd issues
Of identity going for you. Check.
You are minifi'd and easy to read. Check.
We are sorry that we can't be certain
Whether you have submitt'd Poetry.
We are also returning your sentence
"Pope gave Bounce's puppies to his gard'ners."
If you are not a robot, please click here
Or stay on the line please do think of us
In case you ever do write a poem.

Working from Home(r)

Flee to the mountains, for the end of all things is at hand!—
Jones Very to his Greek class at Harvard, Sept. 1838

He wrote about Pope while the nation died.
When they broke thro' the unlock'd study door,
The madman believ'd they were saving him.
Sure, he protest'd 50 years ago;
Now the war is catching up with dodgers.
Pigs made sure to secure his manuscript
Ravings about civil war in England,
Depos'd despots, The Pope as anti-Christ.
Shovel'd rare books to the streets for burning;
Smear'd feces on his photo with Francis;
Forc'd him to eat a toilet paper roll.
He watch'd his dog being shot in the face.
Tortur'd by cell phone muzak on hold;
Strip danc'd with a crucifix up his ass.
They dragg'd him to the local laundromat
Then interrogat'd him for hours.
They book'd him waiting at the DMV
Lucky the former student, a drunken
Dentist, steps forward to administer
Last rites. His publish'r identify'd
The enemy of the people, retain'd
In his name rights future and pluperfect,
Including a catch and kill agreement.
The underground river carried him off.
Peace is the river when it's out of sight.
In the end, it took a lot of rubber
Bullets to kill the man who wrote on Pope.

Silencer
Commentary

An engraving of Pope's unpadd'd chair
Survives from 1862 London
Illustrat'd News. The chair is vacant,
All form thus. Dull silence surrounds the seat
Where friends and sycophants once gather'd
Invit'd to enjoy a warming fire
At the seat of Pope's imagination.
Mostly, the old furniture has been burn'd.
The Parson's Cant, the Lawyer's Sophistry,
Lord's Quibble, Critick's Jest; all end in thee,
All rest in Peace at last, and sleep Nvidia.
This brittle wood allows embellishment
Only between the relic finials:
The carv'd eagle at the top would have been
Expos'd to auditors by Pope's posture,
A bundle of laundry left on a chair;
But hid at his back could he sit up,
An ornamental splat—twin pairs
Of widespread wings parenthesize a sylph.
Pope elevat'd the functional chair
Into a funicular with a view.
Lacking a Yankee aristocracy,
New wealth display'd itself in furnish'd rooms.
There is no chair in Poe's Philosophy
Of Furniture; the rich own two sofas.
His trick swipes the chair out from under Pope.

Dorn wrote poems by the seat of his jeans.
Pants cut from tents tend to tent and not crease.

The music stops; Dulness wins the last seat.

Pope's Seat
A Note

Bathurst nam'd Pope's Seat at Cirencester
Or, rather, repurpos'd the old chapel.
The "bauble" in architectural form
Was the lord's thanks for helping Rake the Park.

MAGA Hating the Left, the Left Hating MAGA
Abhorrence

Jimmy Kimmel ask'd Pope about hatred.
I think I'd read his reply earlier:

 "…you seem to know me much better as a Poet, than as a Man
…Any Mortal is at full Liberty, unanswer'd, to write and print
of me one Year, and blame me another; only I desire him to spare
my Character as an honest Man, over what he can have no private,
much less public, Right, without some personal Knowledge of my
Heart, or the Motives of my Conduct…" (letter to Hill, May 11, 1738).

Stranger, feel free to hate my poetry,
But you only imagine you know me.
Westminster shut up the Northern Star,
Years after the Dunciad buried him
After lengthy Negotiations, Pope
Reduces Aaron Hill to an asterisk.

Gray Poem, No. 14

This is a private poem. Don't read.

To the Writer of the Epitaph

The only way Pope gets in Westminster
Is as a pallbearer for John Gay.
First, he contribut'd the epitaph.
Forever doing the Heavy Lifting.

Annotations

GRAY is the kind of cemetery you tour.
So is James Joyce in a different way.

Walpole's Cat

The rain lets up, I enter the dark house:
the faces of cats rise to the surface,
Exotic fish to feed off my flashlight.

(Looking at Blake's illustration to Thos. Gray's
Ode to Selima.)

Irony

I squeak'd into Oregon confusing
Gay for Gray on the entrance exams then
Jonson with Johnson. But Wharton econ
On Trump's Wiki needs documentation,
Or is he being ironic again?
Did he sit eyes closed every day in class?
Did he side eye the earnest lecturer?
Did he question his professor's degrees
And dream up Trump University fees?
Did he read Hume, Quesnay, and Adam Smith
Or take them for a law firm? Did he read?
Did tiny fingers tweet tinier themes
Or promise to pay off the ghost writers?
Did he hire thugs to change his final grades:
Transaction as degree modality?

Behind Taste

Behind taste, a favored topic of the whole eighteenth century,
[Kant] had discovered an entirely new human faculty, namely Judgment.
         —Hannah Arendt

Pope design'd the Grotto to be the tomb
Of the unknown body without organs.
Part three, the plan to end the judgment
Of god two centuries early, is first
In the abandon'd Dunciad De Form.
If the creator is denied judgment,
Then the MwO is truly
Free to liberate the tombs of poems
Made visible in the likenesses of
Ovid's potato nose and Pope's HarUMPh.
Pope pronounc'd his judgments on the critics,
Who remain in annotat'd prisons
Serving out lifetime sentences books must.
Judgment Day is the end of times; the day
Lasts 50,000 years awaiting bail.
"Content is judgement," Edwardian Dorn.
He didn't live to see the flag plant'd
Upside down outside the judge's house
When the wind held its breath like on the moon.

ARTAUD - A FIGURE of the Poem

TT

Art(aud)'s Self-Autopsy

We wait'd for the perfect solar storm.
Our plans start'd at the galleries,
Say our how are you's to the paintings then
Stroll thro' Oakland maybe bump into lunch
At a table set up on the sidewalk.
The store of gently used books is right next door.
How many meetings did the indispos'd
Pope need to cancel at the last minute?
So I'm stuck at home thinking there will be
Only so many more days to miss you.
Reduc'd to writing this emo lyric.
Just then the mail truck drops into my lap
Artaud's Radio Works (on a Sunday)!
On the first page, Rob Murray invites me:
"To have done with the judgement of god is
the culmination of Artaud's project
to create a new body, one which would
do away with the tired old corporeal
forms…It is here that Artaud's 'body
without organs' emerges for the first
time, 'dancing inside out.'" He'd be censor'd…
Once my eyes adjust to the dark inside,
I pick up "To have done with the judgement
Of god" where the kid left off at Kent.
I have the whole day to decode the script's
De Form'd, and for learning to dance inside
Out, pausing once for a guy davenport

(Fried baloney sandwich and a Snickers)
I miss you, Mathilda. I will give you
My copy of the Anti-Oedipus
To carry for me into the future.
You will see, I have assiduously
Refrain'd from making notes in the margins
This once. I leave the text as I found it,
And reserve my tho'ts for this poem to you.

Epistles from Artaud

Artaud conduct'd business for Judgement's
Broadcast in verse, sending epistles to

Pouey on Dec. 11, 1947
Paulhan on Feb. 10, 1948
Guignard on Feb. 17, 1948
F. Laval on Feb. 20, 1948.

To spit in their eyes with his last good breath.

Grottobiographical Approach

Pope lov'd doctors indiscriminately
Artaud hates every last one of em
Treating the French tongue, "le grand malade"

Fifty one shock treatments June '43-
Dec. '44 broke a vertebra
In his back, bent him into a likeness
Of Pope's deformity. Of Vincent he
Wrote: "No one has ever written, painted,
Sculpted, modeled, built, invented except
Literally to get out of hell." Dies
At the foot of his bed, holding a shoe
Sleepwalked his way out of the infantry
Fear of sleep is being in hell helpless
To dream up a way out. Biographer
Of the sun teen Heliogabalus
The body as a walking tree of will,
Only the face human, survives Ovid

The Egg

The Huhn came first
Then Fassbinder made one movie every 100 days
                    for 13 years dedicating
Desire to Outo.
Very wrote 200 "English" sonnets between
fall 1838 and fall 1839. The voice of
the Holy Ghost came to him, 2,800 lines
in Shakespearean form.
My poem a day over the last three months
                    is chickenshit.
He also wrote, produced, and edited;

did some acting and camera work.

Okay. So now we think we know the Egg.

"Lo! one vast Egg produces human race."

    Instantaneous Divagations:

((I'm a dunce for the thinkers' example

Of the egg stage in BwO.)

John Rich's mime of hatching from an egg

On stage made the Dunciad in Book 3.))

Erase the parentheticals, and this is a love sonnet

Alexander Pope is the most quot'd

And among the least read after Shakespeare,

Whose plays they make us read in junior high.

Zukofsky's barely and widely syndrome

(And the vacation he spent in Stratford)

Are a supreme irony not lost on

The ironist of Twickenham Grotto.

(Henley is in the battle for second.)

Secretly in love with books that exhaust

The initial affair so consuming

I was unmoor'd and never recover'd,

Only surviv'd, contrived to seek her out.

Mistaking Clarel, or the Dunciad,

The Cantos, The Ring of Saturn, for her;

Harboring the wish to write the story

Beyond old age and physical desire

(I'll never see her face. She has no face.)

The Translator (Is Out)

My thot on Artaud rates inexpert fakes
Like Mark Spitzer's forgeries of the Great
French Poets so he could live in Paris
Another week. I don't speak the language
Either, only I am older and you
Are dead. Greensburg's a new Season in hell
Where I still dwell, retired poor and condemned,
Eating and sleeping   surrounded by books.
Having to take Eshleman's word for it
When I read Artaud.

When I read Celine

The times I try to picture the Grotto
In terms of Dave Virilio's bunker—
His concept of constructing a ruin
To protect the countrified border—
"Hitler" overwhelms all constructive thots.
("Stunned by the sudden storm of woes,…
He looks at the havoc spread around him,
Whether he himself is left, and fears
Lest the very ground…may not prove
Treacherous," Jones Very's "Hamlet.")
The invention of fascism required

Cathedrals more massive than ones Pope dreamt.
If Pope wrote in the Grotto, ambient
Piano played on the underground roll,
His seat facing a silent movie Thames.
"'Tis but a part we see, and not a whole."

Alexander Pope Spits

Artaud's choice for opening "To have done"
Is a wild conspiracy theory
Involving the government stockpiling
Schoolboy's sperm to grow soldiers to fight wars.
The playwright is to read this part himself.
Each of the following sections requires
A reader. Next, the pre-Columbian
Dance abolishes the cross and erects
A gigantic horseshoe which men worship.
The third vatic voice reports the research
On Shit, professed by Roger Blin, whose Christ
"Consented to live without a body"
In a ploy to dodge crab louses. All this
Fell to our Fassbinder to make "Flatus,
Or Life Among the Borborygmus."
Part fourth was to pour forth from Paule Thevenin
Speaking over the toots and the voiding;
Artaudian sound effects were language.
(Author's letter to voice actor closes:
"There are those who eat too much and there are

Others who, like me, cannot eat any
Longer without SPITTING." (2/24/1948))
Try superimposing Peri Bathouse,
Or The Art of Stinking in Poetry.
Six lines before the end, Artaud himself
Pronounces "a body without organs"
In the script he is forbidden to speak,
The miracle that flabbergasts us still.

Free Bullets with Today's Purchase of a Gun

The fourth Dunciad prints, as an Appendix, "A Parallel of the Characters
of Mr. Pope and Mr. Dryden," a handy reference for contemporary criticism
of the author's poetry, politics, morals, and religion. It is Pope's crowning
Satire. E.g.:

"an open and mortal enemy of the country"

"only a versifier"

"understood no Greek or Latin"

"does not talk like Homer, but like Pope"

"A little abject thing."

Pope, a Film
Starring Artaud's face over the years.

Why I Hate "Essay on Man," and Tho't I Dislik'd Pope

The Rule the next line rimes may not suspend
Laws which rule out place keeper platitudes
Only the gift'd poets make good sense
Proformas they school themselves to unlearn.
Awful in any age, "Whatever is.
Is right" carpenter'd into "…reason's right,"
And coming from a Catholic—it's treason.
The Whig's in need of Tory De form.
Did I say Whig? Pope's letter changes looks
As easy as its reader Bolingbrook.

The Corrections

The Appendix for the Fourth Edition
Has a section for Pope's own corrections.
I regret I left the cat in the dark
Room when I went to jot the single line,
"CORRECTIONS AFFORD POOR APHORISMS,"
And return'd to bed where she'd been sleeping.
Rime had follow'd me down, expecting to play.
Soon the few birds grow a darkling chorus.
The sound of tomorrow makes Rime's ears twitch.
It's already 7:00 in London.

E-mail to Alexander Pope

Twice
divorced, long retired.
In my leisure, I read for pleasure
      strife, sickness, discontent,
      a perverse jealousy among poets
      since Ovid—-Coleridge
desperate to use Soul in a sentence—-
      Darker Reflections
      Nijinsky's Diary
     God's Scrivener
      John's poems
      Carrington, *Down Below*:
"Every time I got a book off the shelves, I would consult the list,
hoping that its title would not be there: but there it would be
every time." It occurs to me, this stack of bedside books might
be poisoning?
      Art Pepper, *Straight Life*
      (new) The Notebooks of Sonny Rollins

I can live with "Music is a *divine* revelation." (Rollins)

Glenn Gould invented at his piano
Happenings for a downtown department
Store full of inner voices critics feared.

There are two kinds of poets:
great poets,

and those who have yet to realize
they are not great.
In his madness, Frost believed
he was Robert Frost.
The Holy Ghost spoke through Jones Very,
upon hearing Emerson lecture.
Nijinsky believed he was God.
Literature is beyond
hope
that someone who does not know me
will remember me
A literary life
becomes the words, one remove.
Reading Ian Penman
on Fassbinder, and thinking
about Pope.
About Dorn.
"…the messiness remains; he hasn't become a smoothed-out
icon or conventional role model; something in him still resists
such easy appropriation. Too untidy and paradoxical. Difficult
to canonize, difficult to mourn. Difficult to *assimilate.* He is the
opposite of those modernist figures who leave behind a tiny nest
of fragments…the cult of the little and the lost, the sliver and the
fragment."

At last,
Auden shuffling off to church
in his slippers. Faithful
as the cat knows
to call it a day,

follows me to bed
and falls asleep first.
When I wake, in the night,
jot down a word for Pope,
she leaps "overmorrow."

I have followed you home, Pope, like a dog

The notes Gaddis wrote after finishing
A book became the start for the next one.
My father smoked cigarettes like that, Jim
Lit his smoke with the sentence's dying stub.
My tendency is to publish it whole.
Nothing in me of his perfectionist
Dodge of coming up before men's judgment.
Dad never finished once he had begun.

Chiasmus for His Birthday

Wit-constructed mountains he glissades down,
Leaving us the climb without equipment.

FINIS
May 21, 2024

Sources

Antonin Artaud, *Artaud Anthology*, ed. Jack Hirschman (1965).

——————, *Radio Works: 1946-48*, trans. Clayton Eshleman (2022).

W.H. Auden, "Alexander Pope," in *Pope, A Collection of Critical Essays,* ed. J.V. Guerinot (1972).

Stephen Barber, *Antonin Artaud* (2002).

Mavis Batey, *Alexander Pope, The Poet and the Landscape* (2006).

Reginald Berry, *A Pope Chronology*, 1988.

Harold Bloom, ed., *Alexander Pope*, 1986.

The Cambridge Companion to Alexander Pope, ed. Pat Rogers (2007).

Leonora Carrington, *Down Below* (1988).

The Correspondence of Alexander Pope, ed. George Sherburn, vols. III, IV (1956).

Gilles Deleuze and Felix Guattari, *Anti-Oedipus*, trans. Hurley, Seem, and Lane (1977).

Peter Dixon, *The World of Pope's Satires* (1968).

Edward Dorn, *Collected Poems*, ed. Jennifer Dunbar Dorn (2012).

——————, *Derelict Air,* Justin Katko and Kyle Waugh, eds. (2015).

Robert Duncan, "The Trojan Wars Renewed: A Capitulation or The Dunkiad," in *The Collected Books of Jack Spicer*, ed. Robin Blaser (1975).

The Dunciad in Four Books, ed. Valerie Rumbold (2009). A masterpiece of textual scholarship.

The Odyssey of Homer, transl. Alexander Pope, 1880. A gift from Dean Keller.

Dustin Griffin, *Alexander Pope, The Poet in the Poems* (1978).

Joseph Hone, *Alexander Pope in the Making* (2021).

Samuel Johnson, *The Life of Pope,* ed. Jack Lynch, online 23 April 2024.

Maynard Mack, *Alexander Pope* (1985).

——————, *The Garden and The City* (1969).

Marjorie Nicholson and G.S. Rousseau, *"This Long Disease, My Life": Alexander Pope and the Sciences* (1968).

Ian Penman, *Fassbinder Thousands of Mirrors* (2023).

Peter Quennell, *Alexander Pope, the Education of a Genius* (1968).

Ian Sinclair, Review of Edward Dorn's *Collected Poems*, LRB, April 11, 2013.

John Sitter, *The Poetry of Pope's Dunciad* (1971).

Harry M. Solomon, *The Rape of the Text* (1993).

Elizabeth Tebeaux, "Scepticism in Poe's *Essay on Man*," *College Literature*, 1983.

Helen Vendler, *Poets Thinking,* Chapter 1 (2006).

Basil Willey, "Cosmic Toryism," Chapter 3 of *The Eighteenth Century Background* (1940).

"ARE You TRYING to DESCRIBE DORN, Slinger?"

TT

"SILK PADDING SELDOM MADE THE WEAK LINE FINE"